Autobiography/
Anti-Autobiography

Jennifer Bartlett

Copyright © 2014   Jennifer Bartlett

ISBN-13: 978-0-9883891-2-0

Thank you to the editors of the publications in which these poems originally appeared: *The Denver Quarterly, Brooklyn Rail, ESQUE, Eleven Eleven, The c_L newsletter, Wordgathering, Delirious Hem,* and *Beauty is a Verb: The New Poetry of Disability.*

"Anti-Autobiography" was previously published as a chapbook designed by Andrea Baker (SES/Youth-in-Asia Press).

Thank you also to Lisa Jarnot, Andrea Baker, Jeff Hoover, Robert Grenier, Sam Lohmann, Marie and John Stewart, Sheila Black, Michael Northen, Peter Littlefield, Roxann Beck Foley, Lee Bartlett, Melanie Neilson, Susan Bee, Charles Bernstein, Steve Tills and mostly, Jim and Jeffrey Stewart.

Cover Image: Photo by Emma Bee Bernstein, 2005.
Estate of Emma Bee Bernstein © 2014.

Book Designer: Jeremy Luke

Autobiography/Anti-Autobiography
is published by theenk Books,
107 Washington Street, Palmyra, NY 14522:
theekbooks.com or
http://therepublicofcalifornia.com/theenk/theenkBooks.htm

Contents

Autobiography 5

Anti-Autobiography 35

Preface

What is 'my lot' ? What's in 'a lot' ? Thrash round & Curse my Maker—why not ? Or lay the whole circumstance out, exactly as it has been experienced, & may need to be said to be ... because the words are *'different'* but the *Same* as all that, & the humans are here (only (?)) to Tell the Life Story (so that 'That' may come into existence & dwell 'in the flesh', at least temporarily (!)) ... because God is *Jealous* of all the *Fun* we're having down here below, & has elected to *'join the fray'*, the holy maiden Jennifer Bartlett was born !

Jennifer Bartlett 'makes the case'/ testifies to all the actual crap that being born with cerebral palsy entitles her to experience, and what life has been like/*is like* in contemporary America for her—*given her lot*—and then, in the second part of the book ('despite the facts') turns round and *Celebrates Her Existence* anyway: "AWAY WITH ALL THAT !" she cries, petulantly and determinatively (waves her arm), and devotes the 'other half of the book' to her ordinary interested investigations/explorations of what is going on & necessary in her daily life in Brooklyn/New York, as if she were a real/actual/'extraordinary' sentient being (like everybody in a body) determined to 'understand' and attempt to 'know the whole of it'/what each can know from the 'absolute perspective' of each one's own organism:

Into the Tumult ! !

Into which each has been 'thrown'—but then, how/what to say to/*of it* (including love poems, if it comes to that, for some other mortal/human) ... is articulated here admirably, beginning to end !

    a movement spastic
               and unwieldy

    is its own lyric

Well, for god's sake, *of course it is* ! Because of her ... ! (*She dood it, &/or She's done it* ! !) Which these poems demonstrate and prove.

                      —Robert Grenier
                      June 23, 2014

Autobiography

For Nathaniel Tarn and Janet Rodney

This monster, the body, this miracle, its pain, will soon make us taper into mysticism, or rise, with rapid beats of the wings, into the raptures of transcendentalism.

                        from "On Being Ill" — Virginia Woolf

to walk means to fall
to thrust forward

to fall and catch

the seemingly random
is its own system of gestures

based on a series of neat errors
falling and catching

to thrust forward

sometimes the body misses
then collapses

sometimes
it shatters

with this particular knowledge

a movement spastic
                and unwieldy

is its own lyric and
the able-bodied are

tone-deaf to this singing some

    falling

is of its own grace

some

    falling

        rather occurs

out of laziness or distraction

here, the entire frame is shaken

these are the falls

where I tell myself

you shouldn't have fallen

I mean to inflict

while the critic of the world watches

o stupid, stupid world

so that, the mother might
say your child must be angry

because you are disabled

so I told her, your child
must be angry

because you are a bitch

and the children ask
why do you talk like that?

and I ask them
why do you talk like that?

and children grow up
knowing this is ordinary

and when there is silence
all naked

this voice seemingly
corrupted

or absent, so *clarity is*
       and isn't
and this voice is full of longing
to connect

when I speak, it's as though
speaking underwater

the poems are a mere reflection
               of the murky underside

To be crippled means to be institutionalized, infantilized, unemployed, outcast, feared, marginalized, fetishized, desexualized, stared at, excluded, silenced, aborted, sterilized, stuck, discounted, teased, voiceless, disrespected, raped, isolated, undereducated, made into a metaphor or an example. To be crippled means to be referred to as retard, cute, helpless, lame, bound, stupid, drunk, idiot, a burden on society, in/valid. To be crippled means to be discounted as a commodity or regarded as mere commodity.

to be crippled means to have a window
into the insanity of the able-bodied

to be crippled means to
see the world slowly and manically

                 to translate
to record
                 to adapt

to be crippled means to have
access to people's fear

of their own erosion

I wore braces to be more like them
to be *better*

I went to normal schools
because I was normal

I was asked to deny this movement
because this movement wasn't effective enough

I was taught to walk
because walking is always preferable
to not walking

I was taught to walk
so they wouldn't have to reform
their beautiful architecture

and if I couldn't walk fast enough
it was my problem and I was left behind

I was asked not to give birth to children
because they might be like me

those who made fun of me were told
their children would turn out like me

and this was meant to be some form
of kindness or protection

I asked myself to fit
the way they thought I should

so I could have their jobs
and their happy lives

and now I am exhausted
from their stupid asking

from my own stupid asking

I am merely curiosity; your own small freak show. Drag my bones out to Coney Island and feel free to make an example out of me. Perhaps people will pay a nickel to get in. I'm tired of giving the show out for free. Drag me through the field of saints. Bless me, pray for me, or rub my head for good luck. I am the product of bad karma. I am punishment for my mother's aborted able-bodied children. I am the one nature meant to throw away.

main part
primary figure
opposite of the soul
                opening
mere container

the thing that transitions

shelter me

flawed shelter

                unwieldy

spastic soldier

invalid of no legal force

crippled

> *to crook, to bend*

sometimes offensive: a lame or partly disabled person or animal

flawed and imperfect
annulment of the body

empty, vast, wide, hollow
space seemingly unoccupied

in the desert sky
stars and stars and stars

I imagine how we might
go on forever
a black mass, fluttering

trees bowed toward
the bending house

a spring snow is merely to be expected

how to pull the arc of my dying

across the page

how to tell the city (birds) to be quiet
and the sky and

this sky

and buildings thrusting
the nest of the city upward

this world (seemingly) holds enough
for all of us

composed primarily
of water and light

this is my body
I am its light

a mere shadow remains
so that, the body is erased

excepting movement

I am all motion and
this motion is neither weak nor hideous

this motion is simply my own

the near miss
seemingly random

what appears chaos to the casual observer
is rather a neatly composed system of gestures

these accidents reside in me

what looks painful from a distance
is just the body reiterating itself

is it true that the crippled
are much closer to enlightenment

by the mere gesture of
getting through this world

      that longing
that want for silence

these bones as if birds
tiny things that at any moment

could take off in flight

breaks the spine like any other

small curve in the back

you rest your hand there

pull from the chair
to which they insist she is *bound*

crack into the center

unfolds origami limbs
a mere semblance of paper

uncurls crooked legs
thrusts into the center

can one be exploited when one is complicit in the exploitation

I was born dead.

It is said that those who remember their own births are liars.

I do not remember this event -- it is merely a story presented to
                                                                                               me
that, in the retelling, becomes part of memory.

The facts are superfluous; one is born, one dies
how one *arrives* is without meaning.

takes the ticket out
of the purse

looks at the ticket

puts the song on
takes the song off

returns the ticket to the purse

yells at the social worker

looks toward the cold field
where the geese

startle and lift

like their return
this will all be over soon

takes the ticket out
of the purse

looks at the ticket

puts the song on
takes the song off

returns the ticket to the purse

looks out on the field among
the geese, this will all be over soon

phones the nurse, phones the friend
phones the clinic, yells at the nurse

people look, look at her,
look at the field,

the geese *lifting*

yells at the nurse
yells at the field

blames the geese

takes the ticket out
of the purse

looks at the ticket

puts the song on
takes the song off

returns the ticket to the purse

looks out to the field
among the geese

there is a body
and this body is gross

it drools and itches
       begs
desires and desires

it shits, pisses, bleeds, eats

the machines now do these things for it

the mind is left
to wander and drift

there is a soul and sometimes this
soul kills

often a pattern is flawed
you could almost miss it

the silence among the reeds
a curtain shut against cadences

the train draws its pattern through the country

how people and birds
struggle and thrive

through the swamp, an endless journey
large birds settle in the sludge

egrets, swans, ducks, cormorants
theirs is a language written through light

something that floats and disperses in radiation

the expanse of my body

my crippled self
how I wish I might be the ocean

all summer we made paper
beneath the ghost of a library

the light filtering through
basement window splaying

on the children's abandoned artwork
making and making with abandon

our hands knee deep in

all living things need a cover

how about the tent of my fluffy pink sweater

how about the ocean

man is so fond of water
a lyric to save the sea

a garden of rocks, silence

I will do anything to escape this canvassing for boats

dear dad

are you done with the poem
is there really a poem

or

are you merely trying to speak
in a dialect I understand

this is to say

leave me be or
I need silence

assuming birds have hearts
do birds have heart attacks

do birds' hearts ache

does your heart still ache

The cat had the pink
thing in its mouth
trapped on the rug.

I saw it moving,
the opening and closing
of the miniature yellow beak.

You hovered over it
trying to make sense of death;
the still glued eyes
pasted windows looking inward.

How I might lift the dying bird
and replace it under
the trees.

My Catholic hope that
the mother will be filled
with longing, so that she will
not abandon it.

I, the surrogate, might offer
the child worms, insects, leaves.

But, who am I to decide the fate of anything?

The sun rears her unlikely head.
In this late spring,
I walk past rubber black boots decorated
With brightly colored umbrellas
In a useless attempt to block the rain.

Up the subway to 14th street
Around the corner to 12th
I climb to the tenth or the eighth floor
Depending on your bodily condition.

I keep vigil over this resting.
My body is a candle, glowing
Until you make the transition
Back into or out of this life.

This is among the things that could happen.
This is among the things that happened.
For now, you reside in imposed silence.
Dying is just another commodity and

The soul wants routine.
The soul wants sameness, boredom.
The soul wants *letting go.*

Over us, the palmed stars.

Anti-Autobiography

I'm not interested in myself -- that's just this guy who sits here drinking coffee and making a fool of himself. If only a self got posited in a poem we may as well be having lunch somewhere and not bothering with poems. A self that is transformed through language, however, interests me, though that already includes the reader as we are all part of a shared language. It seems to me to become reductive, however, exactly at that point where you focus on the self and thus end up with poetry of personality, and that exhausts itself as soon as the personality exhausts itself.

— Michael Palmer (Talking Poetry)

The prevalence of the photographs is especially interesting in light of the participation of the workshop poem in the "optical illusion" of the first person; it is as if the editors go so far as to distrust even the I of the poem and so must reinforce the false realism by having "real" people staring back at the reader.

— Lee Bartlett (What is Language Poetry?)

Every girl's object relations.
—Peter Littlefield

Is it true that the west means space?

that *fragmented* space
                that scattering

the moths are unruly this year
throughout the trees
a cocoon of leaves

[*sometimes you have to walk into the forest*]

                can this happen?
and this
                and this?

Is it true that one can live in new york and be a west coast poet?

                that night, all night
                I watched you sleep
                dreaming in a landscape
                of extinct animals

        I want the morning to erase this night.

I, too, know what it is like to want to sit in a chair of a certain color.

                crazy eye, geese balloon and
                sometimes the visiting is good
                but seemingly endless

in these *dying trees*
webs of moths
dying branches

o ugly eastern sky
o sleep o teenagers
o solace o nameless lake
o children in the bedroom
playing marbles/that joy

if you know what is going to happen, it is not an experiment

                         email nathaniel
                         send postcard to kate and max
                         books and notebook for james

           happiness is a sunny day

Jen, I'm just handing you this in case you want it.

             the teenagers still on the lake
             now they will have to ask
             the stars for guidance
             the small children playing marbles
             adults in with cribbage

(360) 481-2019

perhaps the title is: *for james, on his 28th birthday, i love you*

             [for, I am not today without conflicted feelings
                     in preparing the text]

I wish the teenagers would come back now
for it is officially dark.

yes, james, I'm sure someone loves you & you should give it a five
beat rest
                       to find our way

I took out my compass

Then, too, the writing of the essay was personal agony. Where we bear public testimony (,) we face not only the community of thoughtful men and women who are concerned with the good, but facing the open forum we face mean and stupid men too.

[reading this some fifteen years later]

[here insert Julia's plastic purple ponies on the airplane to russia] *sometimes everything is illuminated*

simply glowing

[but this can only occur while one is drunk
and in a taxi cab on the williamsburg bridge
after 11 pm in pleasant weather]

that startling

When I looked out the window, I heard a crash. I saw the motorcycle and the body flying through the air, and the other motorcycle stopped. I saw a figure walk up to the body and the figure didn't bend down, just walked away. There was utter silence in that moment, at that place. And the ambulance moved away in slow motion and it did not turn its lights on.

this line is so fragmented
          when I have to cross it
will emma be there to greet me

Dear Jim, Mom called. I thought she was going to offer to pay for your airline ticket, but she told me to talk you out of going to Guatemala because she read on the internet that it is very dangerous. We agree that there are Mayan temples in Mexico. Call her.

I have been joyous.

>August 22, 2010
>Sam & Michaela
>4025 SE Taylor
>Portland, OR 97214

I ~~at this point~~ am not available to anyone.

>Chlamydia
>Gonorrhea
>Scabies
>Herpes
>Syphilis
>Crabs
>& so on
>& so forth

and how he had a whale upon his shirt
and how he wrote about the ocean and

how his voice mirrored the mirroring of the ocean and

how *these ocean birds make boats of their bodies* and how
he made a boat across my body

how he comes (a)part

and flutters
like a dying thing

    then the quiet water

and the frogs sing against half-light
the swimmer's arms turning to branches

    the quiet quiet water
        as a measure of

your hand in mine
all hearing recedes

into the grey wings
upon nothingness

August 24, 2010
Radiant Child
Film Forum
10:00 PM

A 32:00 minute telephone conversation beginning at Houston and 6th Ave. Ending at 14th street and 6th Ave.

Saint Vincent's Hospital

I walk through the village absent of the usual crowd. It's a Tuesday! And all the queens are asleep.

and here is *once upon a tart*
and here is the church where Tommaso
and I went to the Italian feast my 21st summer
and here is where I saw *Paris is Burning*
and here is the apartment I dreamed of
and here is where Jane King broke my heart
and here is the bookstore that closed
and here is the studio of the Japanese painter
who Rachel worshipped
and here is where I kissed John
and here is where I bought the Alessi coffee pot
for Jim's 34th birthday
and here is *twelve chairs* [which I think Manon's father
owns, but I'm not sure]
and here is the place I've never eaten
and here is the corner where I met Jim
and here is where Charles had his sixtieth birthday
                          party
and here is where they do not have baby food
and here is where we paid too much for the bagel
and here and here and here

How do I unravel myself?

45

1. Dept. of Health called today. Some I know well enough to have my phone number tested positive for syphilis and I have to go in to get tested. Gotta

2. tell S. tonight. That will be fun. Remember what happened when you were here?

3. Have I mentioned cowboy? Fourth date yesterday ....knows S.

4. Fucks like a madman with his boots on and thinks I'm gorgeous.

5. Doesn't look too bad for weather.....but seriously, I've been looking forward to the top off road trip for ages and it's raining here and the last thr

6. I was bad, really bad... So I made my stop and before you know it 10 guys are there [this portion of the text has been censored to protect the innocent].

when all the men come off the water
when the sailing is done
               where the wind resides
more full of flames   and voices

when we try to capture
       and are, ourselves, held

where this wind resides
most will come off the water

from the blue of the sky to her
[where] *she would bring down the little birds*

             [to rest in her palms]

*I took out my compass
but it was useless here*

> August 4, 2009
> The Beach @
> Governor's Island
> 8 PM

mourning is a cruel country where I am no longer afraid

Mom, I came in for two things:
        a. give me some sugar
        b. can I sleep in the living room

a. yes
b. no

August 9, 2009
St. Luke's-Roosevelt Hospital
10th and 59th
10:02 AM

In order to go to sleep, you must build a canoe. In order to go to sleep, you must put yourself in a canoe. You must launch from the shore, and from this shore, you must leave all objects and people behind. Sometimes one person can go in the canoe to help you along. Only one person is allowed. This person cannot be a lover or a child. As you get further from the edge, you will have to commit to cutting the string that binds you. So, remove the scissors from your dress and cut the line. Cut the line.

down twelve flights of stairs
left of sixth
turn on mulberry
christopher walken and a very tall woman
magnolia bakery   *get my things, I'm leaving*
bookstore   *pull the car around*
small intimate corner park

boutique 1   *people can sometimes reside in*
boutique 2   *the intensive care unit for years*
boutique 3

this apartment means *green living*   *often longing has a system*
the empanada bakery   *but not a map*
two boots -- buffalo chicken pizza

julian schnabel's big old pink castle of a house   *what purpose do*
the river   *we have for*
westbeth   *this body*

boutique 4
boutique 5   *this is my love letter to letting go*
boutique 6

turn left on dirty, dirty 6th avenue   *this meandering*

The modern denial of death does not explain the extent of the lying and the wish to be lied to: [for] it does not touch on the deepest dread.

August 9, 2009
The Red Heroine
McCarren Park
Nightfall

What I take of yours is mine, what I leave of yours is what I seem to be selling.

dear inflection

o ocean, o place
o little blue house, o *gleaming*
o long road of indiana
o silence, o longing

peter is my littleboat that i get in and row around

the persona is erased
so that, this could be, not my autobiography per se,
but the autobiography of any girl

Jennifer Bartlett was born in the San Francisco Bay Area and educated at the University of New Mexico, Vermont College, and Brooklyn College. She is the author of *Derivative of the Moving Image* (UNM Press 2007) and *(a) lullaby without any music* (Chax 2012). Bartlett also co-edited, with Sheila Black and Michael Northen, *Beauty is a Verb: The New Poetry of Disability*. Bartlett has received fellowships from the New York Foundation for the Arts, Fund for Poetry, and the Dodd Research Center at the University of Connecticut.

She is currently writing a full-length biography of the poet Larry Eigner. She lives in Brooklyn, NY, with the writer Jim Stewart and their son, Jeffrey Stewart.

www.ingramcontent.com/pod-product-compliance
Lightning Source LLC
Chambersburg PA
CBHW031430290426
44110CB00011B/597